Alma

Daughters with Narcissistic Mothers

Dealing with a Self-Absorbed mother and Healing from Narcissistic Abuse. Recovering from Psychological Abuse and Emotionally Immature Parents

Contents

10

Recognizing The Problem-The Narcissistic Mother

Many people are in the dilemma of choosing between their dreams or their parents' dreams. This problem is quite normal in the teenagers to today's generation. And I don't blame them as their parents are merely responsible of expecting them to chase their dreams instead of letting their children or daughters be independent.

The problem in the parent-kid relationship occurs when the parent starts to enforce her positive characteristics in her child. Normally, most of the parents do not torture the kid constantly to be perfect in all situations but there are some parents who cannot tolerate bad characteristics in their children, especially if they are the epitome of perfection in their eyes. Self-obsessed parents usually torture their kids mentally, as well as physically (in rare cases) to get rid of their bad characteristics (which of course, is a natural part of growing up) and bear with the positive characteristics like them. Not everyone can be perfect, especially the growing children or the children in their teenage but, most of the people or the parents fail to realize that.

In the recent years, we have observed many child depression cases emerging in the society. For some parents, it is quite against the cultural norms or is a shame to have children with certain bad characteristics. They have the concept that their children should always reflect their positive characteristics and their independence and freedom is a threat to them. Such parents look down upon their children and try to mold them in their personality, rather than nurturing their own personalities. These parents are clearly self-centered of self-obsessed about themselves and want their children to possess their qualities and positive personality characteristics, even if it cost them their children's mental peace.

The parents who are self-centered and self-obsessed are more likely, suffering from narcissism. They fall under the category of narcissistic parents and are knowingly or unknowingly suffering from narcissistic personality disorder. But, to actually know what narcissistic personality disorder is, you need to know the origin and the meaning of the term, 'narcissism'. Narcissistic personality disorder is not rare among the parents. In the recent year, this personality disorder has grown, especially into the parents of young or teenage children. Firstly, I am going to discuss with you briefly about what actually is narcissism and narcissistic personality disorders and how and why are the parents, especially the mothers suffering from the narcissistic personality disorder.

What Does The Term 'Narcissism' Mean?

Narcissism is the term, or rather a concept that shows the pursuit of utmost gratification or self-obsession from the egoistic or vanity admiration of one's perfect personality or attributes. In simple words, it is the admiration or a keen interest in one's own perfection, positive characteristics and attributes. It is not necessary if the person possesses perfect personality attributes or not, this term reflects the deep intent of self-obsession for one's personality or attributes. In most cases, the term narcissism also refers to having a clear obsession about one's physical features or about one's physically appearance or beauty.

In a psychological view, it is the term that refers to an abnormal self-love, involving selfishness, lack of care or empathy from anybody else and a constant need to be admired every now and then. If you have somebody in your social circle who admires himself a lot and constantly finds reasons to be admired, then he or she is suffering from narcissism. It is the self-centeredness that can arise in the personality due to the failure of distinguishing oneself from external things, either as a feature or the characteristic of a mental disorder, or in very young infants or babies.

Origin Of The Term 'Narcissism'

This term is originated from the Greek mythology. In the mythology, the young Narcissus became self-obsessed or fell in love with his own reflection or the image in the water pool. Narcissism originally became a theory in 1914 when Sigmund Freud wrote an essay about it.

People suffering from this cultural problem are likely to have narcissistic personality disorder. Now, I am going to brief you about the narcissistic personality disorder before I move on to the term 'Narcissistic parents' or the, 'Narcissistic mothers'.

Narcissistic Personality Disorder

The other term for narcissism is megalomania. In simple words, the one suffering from megalomania has a narcissistic personality disorder. The narcissistic personality disorder is the term which refers to having long term effects or a pattern of egoistic or abnormal behavior that can be characterized by uncontrollable feelings of self-obsession and self-importance. The person suffering from the narcissistic personality disorder is simultaneously suffering from the lack of empathy and the need to be admired every now and then, whether on her physical appearance or on her distinctive personality.

The treatments of the narcissistic personality disorder have not been classified but therapeutic sessions with the psychological professionals have been successful in some extent in eliminating the narcissistic personality disorder in people, especially in parents.

Nowadays, a huge number of people are suffering from narcissistic personality disorder. The narcissistic personality disorder affects them as a parent and has a huge impact on their relationship with their children. Now, I am going to brief you about the narcissistic parents or rather, the narcissistic mothers who have affected their children's personalities due to this personality disorder.

Introduction To Maternal Narcissism

The narcissistic parent or a narcissistic mother is the one who is suffering from the common narcissism personality disorder or narcissism. If you talk about the behavior of the narcissistic parents, or more specifically, the narcissistic mother, they are typically close to their children. They are more emotionally and mentally attached to their children and possess a threat from the independence of the children. They are possessive and exclusive about their children and anything that they do against their will poses a threat to their narcissistic personality.

The narcissistic mothers are extremely unfair to their children and their freedom as they think that the children are merely born to fulfill their wishes and it is important that they possess the positive characteristics of them and admire them to be the best mother. Typically, a narcissistic mother wants a carbon copy of herself as a child and wants to be superior than her child in every aspect of life.

A narcissistic mother tries to control the independence, freedom and the actions of her child, especially the daughter by emotional, mental or physical abuse. Little do they know, it affects the psychological growth and the mental development of the growing child. A narcissistic mother adversely affects the social, moral and ethical behaviors and values of her kid or daughter. Some narcissistic mother try to mold their daughters or the children into a character where they are only allowed to live to fulfill their wishes and desires.

A narcissistic mother often has a low self-esteem. They feel vulnerable if their personality faults are exposed to their children or daughters. Instead of admitting the mistakes, a narcissistic mother blames her child or her daughter and disowns her daughter if she poses a threat to her self-centered personality. A narcissistic mother does not like to get her decisions about her daughter rejected and she has an excuse ready for every mistake that she makes while bringing up her daughter. A narcissistic mother is self-absorbed, with a lack of empathy and flexibility, needed to raise a daughter or a child. Child rising often means adjusting your personality and your personal interests according to the child but the narcissistic mothers are not open to this idea.

Characteristics of a Narcissistic Mother

The Decisions of a Narcissistic Mother Are Always Deniable

Everything that a narcissistic mother does is deniable. She always has an excuse ready whenever she makes a mistake in raising her daughter or her child. Cruelty is regarded as the mother's way of showing love. Hostile and aggressive acts and reactions are considered as thoughtful in the eyes of a narcissistic mother. Slander and criticism are paraded or regarded as a concern towards her daughter or her child. She only wants her child to do what she says as she thinks that her decisions are the best for her child.

A narcissistic mother does not appreciate her daughter or her son. For instance, if her child comes running to her to show or tell her something good that he has done, she will shut him up by comparing him to the her other children and will regard the act as unnecessary or of low importance. And if she does not do that, she will definitely act cruel to her child to make her/him recognize that the act is inappreciable.

A narcissistic mother is always comparing her child's deeds to the other children to constantly remind her child that she/he should be as perfect as them or her. It does not necessarily mean scolding her child. She will just use a harsh tone to congratulate or to show gratitude, which can mentally destroy her child or can take away her/his mental peace and joy. Moreover, the look of her face and the envy in her eyes can adversely affect a growing child.

Abusiveness is a part of a narcissistic mother's personality. She will accuse her child for her wrong decisions and will find an excuse every time she makes a mistake. But, she won't do it in public. The actions of a narcissistic mother are completely secretive. She will abuse her child emotionally when no one is looking around.

A Narcissistic Mother Violates Her Child's Boundaries

A narcissistic mother violates her child's boundaries. For instance, she gives away the things of her child without her child's consent. Moreover, she takes away the food plate from in front of her child even if he has not completed eating his dinner. She can take or use her child's property whenever she likes and she isn't guilty about it. Furthermore, a narcissistic mother invades her child's privacy.

She has a habit of going through her child's things regularly without having consent. A narcissistic mother goes through her child's personal diary, conversations, emails and letters even though a child is not comfortable with her doing that. And the worst fact about the narcissistic mother is that she will dig deep in your heart and will look for negative information so that she can use it against you when it's the right time.

Even if a child stops her, she will do things against her child's will and wishes. For instance she will constantly nag about her child's wishes and choices. If her child dresses according to her own choice, she will nag about it and even when wearing makeup and clothes that are age inappropriate. She will constantly invade her child's privacy by not allowing her child to date. Even if her daughter does date somebody, she will keep certain disturbing and compromising terms, rules and conditions.

In short, a narcissistic mother is so close and possessive about her child that she ridicules her child's independence and freedom. She will try hard to stop her child from becoming independent and free. She wants her child to depend on her for their whole life.

A Narcissistic Mother Do Favoritism

A narcissistic mother constantly chooses one child over the other children and it is a common symptom of a narcissistic parental personality disorder. A narcissistic mother is always in favor with the most liked child. She gives privileges to that child. No matter how her other children do well in studies, she will always regard her favorite child in being the best daughter or the son one could ask for.

But, that is only valid if her golden child does whatever she says. Once he/she stops listening to her, then he is like the other children to her. This habit creates hatred among the siblings and one child has eternal love for her/his mother and the other children hate her for being unbiased. A narcissistic mother will foster that child division by prioritizing the golden child and doing the best only for him.

Moreover, she can also use the golden child to abuse the other children physically. For instance, she can indirectly tell the golden or her favorite child to beat the other children while playing so that she does not have to do that by herself. This is the result of having a low self-esteem and being egoistic. Choosing a golden or a favorite child is common when a mother is suffering from a narcissistic personality disorder.

A Narcissistic Mother Undermines

The accomplishments and the success of the child are only acknowledged by a narcissistic mother to the extent where she can take the whole credit for her child's success. Any accomplishment, success or a good deed from which she cannot take the credit is harshly ignored, unacknowledged or is of no importance to her. For instance, if her child is on stage and she is not getting the attention of the audience to herself at all, she prevents the event or walk straight out of the hall as she cannot tolerate someone getting all the attention while she is present.

To make her feel better, she can sometimes disregard her child and tell him that he could have done better like the other children. She will disrespect and embarrass her child for not giving his best. If she cannot to do under the social pressure, she will deliberately try to steal hid child's spotlight and will try to be the center of attention so that she can take all the credit and get admired by the audience.

She will not support her child's opportunities or achievements in which she has no hands in. She will try to persuade her child that his dreams and choices are useless and will steal his joy of accomplishing something that he always wanted to achieve. She will constantly persuade her child that whatever he has done is tarnished and nothing to be proud of. She will not embarrass a child directly for his success. Instead, she will use that harsh tone and hopeless look to make you feel depressed and wrong about your career decisions.

A Narcissistic Mother Denigrates And Degrades

A narcissistic mother criticizes, demeans and degrades her child in public to be a better person in front of everyone. For instance, she will degrade her child and criticize him upon his mistakes in front of a person, especially if that person is blaming the child for something. Even if the child has been mistreated by someone, she will still put the blame on her child. This behavior can mentally destroy the child.

But, this does not mean that she regards the other person to be right about anything. She just wants to show her child that he will never be right and will never be perfect like her. She is least concerned about the other people and providing justice to her child. All she wants is attention and a few praising words to make her feel better at life.

She will definitely generalize barbs in a sweet and a caring tone. She will criticize her child about not doing enough, about not being enough, about not being perfect and about not doing his 100% and she will do it in a gentle way so that he doesn't get to be the victim. She will always try to play the victim card by speaking about her tragedies and the issues.

She will always complain about no one being there for her and no one taking care of her. It is disgusting as she is talking about herself rather than being there for her child. This is the peak of self-centeredness. She will always complain about the selfishness and the lack of empathy in people and will not note her actions. She will combine the deniability with criticism to make her child feel bad and ashamed of his actions.

She will make her child realize that he does not mean anything to her and will praise the person who tried to degrade you or who tried to defame you. She will pass unspoken messages to her child so that he feels little or no importance of himself in the house. Moreover, she will support the other person who hurt her child to be the most superior one in the house.

She ignores, discounts and minimizes her child's personal experiences and opinions. The child's decisions and career options will constantly be degraded and put off by denials and accusations of doing good ever. Whatever the child does will be ignored by a narcissistic mother, through smirks, exclamations, exaggerated laughs and amused sounding. After that, she will make sure to inform the child that everyone that he has ever said to her was ignored or was not listened by her.

A Narcissistic Mother Makes Her Child Look Crazy

If a child will try to confront her upon her actions, a narcissistic mother will make her child look crazy. She will address to her child in a gentle tone that he has a very vivid imagination and that he will never be able to achieve anything with this attitude. She will constantly make her child feel like she does not know about a thing that he is talking about. She will claim not to remember any occurred event even if that event happened in the past nor will she admit that she might have forgotten the event. She will gaslight her child, which is the common practice done by all the emotional abusers.

The child's perceptions are continuously undermined so that he can end up having no decisions, intuitions and decisions of his own. This helps a narcissistic mother control her child. She brainwashes her child so that he does not have any mind left to think of his own. She does not trust on her child's memory or his addressed events. She ignores her child's capability and the power to think and this makes the child, a better victim for the narcissistic mother to attack.

The routine of a narcissist mother includes gas lighting her child regularly. She will tell her child uprightly that he is unstable or insinuate purposely so that her child can be more co-operative and vulnerable to overlapping depression. She constantly scolds her child for being unrealistic, oversensitive, vulnerable and hysterical. But, she talks to her child when he isn't that angry or is trying to cope with a severe home burn out. She will try to talk her child into thinking that he is being unreasonable. She might even call out names to her child and call him being psychotic or neurotic.

One she has made her child an emotional wreck with less mental stability; she will address her child's problem with everybody else and gain sympathy from the people by playing the victim card. She will cry in front of the others for her child being angry with her, irrationally. She will create an image in front of the people that her child hurts her and that he needs a proper psychological treatment before he loses his mind. And, indicates that there everything has slipped from her hands and there's absolutely nothing that she can do about her child. Hence, gaining a lot of sympathy and attentions which she loves to get.

Soon enough, the narcissistic mother shows lack of empathy towards her child. For instance, she gets absolved herself of her child's responsibility, implying that nothing is wrong with her but with her child. She often plays a role of a doting mother so that no other person can believe her child. Moreover, she can even move take the other family members and friends far from you, implying to them that he has a psychological issue.

A Narcissistic Mother Is Envious

A narcissistic mother envies her child. For instance, many narcissistic mothers compete with their children and compare themselves with their daughters and daughters-in law. Moreover, she continuously point out the imperfections and flaws in her daughter or the daughter-in-law.

She competes with her daughter sexually and envies

her for wearing good clothes and applying a good makeup. For that reason, she might go too far in competition and can even try to hurt her child physically. Moreover, the narcissistic mothers might also destroy her children's marriages or relationships with their spouses. She might even interfere in her child's life when her grandchild is born.

A Narcissistic Mother Lies

A narcissistic mother lies a lot to her child and the people surrounding you to create contradictions and conflicts between the people and between happy relationships. To undermine her child's credibility, she will definitely lie about her child's relationship with her and the other people so that no one can approach him at the first place. A narcissistic mother will constantly inflate herself to get the eyes and ears towards her.

She makes sure that the other people believe her and not her child. For instance, she will lie deliberately and in a sophisticated manner that is hard to lie. Even if she is confronted to tell a lie, she has many escape ways to defend herself. She might even. She might even tell her child's response in advance to the audience so that the people do not listen to her child. It is very difficult for a child to prove her guilty and dishonest, especially in front of his friends and close relatives.

A Narcissistic Mother Wants To Be The Center Of Attention All The Time

A narcissistic mother craves for attention and this is the need of every narcissistic on earth. She decides the house rules so that she can retain perfectionism in the house and get praised by people for keeping the house clean and neat, when actually her child is doing all the house chores.

Moreover, to gain sympathy and the attention, she might create bizarre occasions so that she can cry about a dead family member and can enjoy the spotlight for a few hours. A narcissistic mother will love to steal the attention on any event special to her child, even if it is her child's birthday party. She often comes uninvited to her teenage son's or daughter's friend birthday party and will try to steal the attention of the people by creating a drama or a scene.

Entertaining a narcissistic mother is hard. She gets ragged or agitated when her child does something without her consent or without her getting involved. She just cannot take the answer as a 'no' when she asks her child to go somewhere.

However, some narcissistic mother, when they become old tries to fake a diseases or illness so that they can have immediate response and attention from her child. After she has been successful, she keeps complaining endlessly to her child. Some narcissistic mothers fake the Alzheimer's disease so that they can divert their children's minds towards her.

A Narcissistic Mother Manipulates Her Child's Emotions

A narcissistic mother constantly pins her child emotionally so that he can become emotionally unstable and an emotional wreck. She constantly reminds him of the bad things that have happened to him so that he might never be able to overcome the emotional trauma.

She teases her child in a tormenting way to make him even more sensitive towards the life tragedies. And she will enjoy the distressed and hurt face of her child. A smile will always be there on her face when she talks to her child about his life tragedies and the blunt trauma which he is going through. A narcissistic mother loves to see his child getting hurt. In short, she is feeding off her child's pain to feel good about her life.

A narcissistic mother also cries in front of her child and complains about everyone who tries to hurt her.

She creates an image in the child's mind that she wants to die and does not want to live longer. Now, imagine the mental state of a growing child who's been hearing death wishes.

The Six Faces Of Maternal Narcissism

A narcissistic mother has six faces or six types. Each face or the type of maternal narcissism is briefly describes below.

The Flamboyant Extrovert

The is the narcissistic mother about whom drama serials and movies are made. She is like a star mother or a perfect mother to the public, except her family members and her child. In fact, she is an expert public entertainer. She is socially active, takes part in conversations, gives wise opinions about certain matters and loved by the other mothers or parents.

She listens to everybody outside her house but secretly fears her intimidate children and her spouse.

In front of the public, she displays her personality and her character as an epitome of perfect motherhood. Every mother notices her and her efforts towards her child. She's widely noticed by the public and is fun to hang out with. Moreover, she creates a fake image of herself that she is always there for her child, when in reality she is not. She implies to the public that she is always there to support and counsel her child, when in reality, she just envies her daughter or her son. It is not difficult for her to keep playing two different roles as the narcissistic people are often double standards people. They are very nice on the outside and very hideous from the inside.

Many people love her but her child and her spouse despise the masquerade that she keeps on to entertain the people. And in fact, her family or her children do not matter to her. A narcissistic mother is very egoistic and self-centered. She won't take an actual interest in her child's studies and career unless it's going to get her the public fame and the credit. She only cares about her performance to the world. All she wants to get, is attention. She does not care about her child unless he's an important character in her role play to the world.

The Accomplishment Oriented

This narcissistic mother is always running after the success and grades of her child. She does not care about the mental stability of a child. Instead, she wants her child to score the highest. This type of narcissistic mother is very accomplishment oriented. In her opinion, success is what gets you fame and attention. That is why, she wants her child to get good grades so that she can take all the credit.

This type of narcissistic mother runs after reputable degrees and colleges for her child. No, she does not care for the future well-being of her child. Instead, she wants to be praised for raising a child who can get elected to one of the most reputed colleges in the world.

But, if her child does not accomplish her pre-set goals she becomes angry and is agitated. Due to this reason, she feels embarrassed because of her child. She pushes and forces her child to do even better till his grades are enough to get her the needed attention from the world.

Once her child has accomplished something she takes all the due credit and she does not feel bad about it. She flaunts about the fake efforts that she has to put in her child in order to achieve the goals. Children despise such narcissistic mothers who often tend to forget the mental stability of their children and only want them to score higher in school or college.

The Psychosomatic

A narcissistic mother who uses the physical pain, aches and the illness to draw attention of her child is known as the psychosomatic mother. She can even fake the illness to get the people to notice her. She does not care about those around her. She just wants to feel better by getting all that attention and care.

Moreover, this type of narcissistic mother creates an image that no one is suffering from a medical disease more than her and that this disease is making her want to die. She creates an illusion that no person on earth can be sicker than her. She will give a shut up call to anyone who contradicts with her statement.

The Addicted

Some mothers who are addicted to any drug or even to drinking alcohol are regarded as narcissistic mothers. It is because they keep their addiction above their children. They are not bothered if the drug abuse or the alcohol addiction is causing harm to the offspring or to the fetus in the womb.

Moreover, they do not raise the children as they

should. This lack of empathy and motherhood can be pretty harsh or tough on the kids. They won't know whom to go to when depressed or distressed. The first priority of an addicted narcissistic mother is her drug addiction or her addiction of drinking the alcohol. In fact, some narcissistic mothers can even sell their newly born babies in order to get the cash for the drugs or for the alcohol.

The Secretly Mean

The secretly mean narcissistic mother can have a very bad effect on their children. They are two-faced mothers. They are very good, kind, loving and caring to their children in public but are very cruel and abusive at home. These mixed signals for the child can make him emotionally unstable and a total emotional wreck.

They are nice to the kids in people so that they can have a tag of the 'best mother' on them. But, at home they abuse their children emotionally and physically so that they can feed off their pain. These narcissistic mothers should be immediately reported to the authorities so that a affected children can have stress-free lives. Due to this narcissistically odd behavior, a child cannot anticipate the next move of his mother and end up having a daunting or a confusing image of his mother's love. He does not know whether to trust her or to not.

The Emotionally Needy

The emotionally needy narcissistic mothers are those who want the most emotional attention from their children and from the people. An emotionally needy narcissistic mother shows the characteristics of being vulnerable. They showcase the fake emotional trauma that they are going through so that they can have their children and the other people by their side. She pities herself in front of the public so that she can get all the attention that she needs. An emotionally needy narcissistic mother does not nurture her child, instead, she wants her child to nurture her with care, love, attention and respect 24/7.

Moreover, an emotionally needy narcissistic mother teases or tortures her child and cries about it in front of the other people when her child does not pay attention to her or does not treat her right. This is wrong on so many levels as during the growing age, a child needs her mother. A mother is the building block of his life. If he won't have his mother to rely on, he will obviously find a stranger to receive the missing love, care and attention. However, narcissistic mothers are not concerned about the social gathering of their children. All they want is the due credit and appreciation for raising a child with commendable intellectual capacity.

Statistics On Narcissistic Personality Disorder

Narcissistic personality disorder is prevailing in the ever-growing population of the world, especially in the population of United States. Narcissistic personality disorder can be diagnosed by certain therapies, rehabilitation sessions and treatments, but the problem is that a lot of people, teenagers and specially the parents fail to consult a psychological professional.

A lot of cases have been reported regarding the narcissistic personality disorder and a lot of people are consulting the psychological professionals to get out of this disorder. Narcissistic personality disorder is not inherited or an in-born disorder. Instead, the people develop it over time due to the inferiority complex or due to the societal pressure. The people with narcissistic personality disorder, especially the parents of the children as they have to nurture and raise the children according to the cultural norms.

Narcissistic personality disorder was the subject of many researchers in their studies. So far, they have gathered little data based upon the various cases of narcissistic personality disorder and the types of faces of the maternal or paternal narcissism. Here is the statistical data or findings of the carried out results.

United States Statistics On Narcissistic Personality Disorder

According to the data gathered, approximately 0.5% of the general population of the United States is suffering from narcissistic personality disorder. Moreover, 2-16% of the population who is seeking help from the medical professionals is reported to have a narcissistic personality disorder.

Almost 6% of the forensic population is suffering from narcissistic personality disorder. But, most of the narcissistic traits present in the general population and in the forensic population are not referred as actual narcissistic personality disorder. Actual narcissistic traits are found in the veterans or the people in military. Almost 20% of the military population is suffering from the narcissistic personality disorder. All six types of narcissistic issues have been reported to the psychological professionals by the military population.

In United States of America, more than 17% of the population of the medical students (first year) is suffering from narcissistic personality disorder. The founder of the IRHRPPE (Institute of Relational Harm Reduction and Public Pathology Education), Sandra L. Brown describes in her online journal at almost 60 million people living in the United States are suffering from the narcissistic traits of the people or the family members around them.

She further says that there are at least 304 million people who are suffering from narcissistic personality disorder in the United States. However, this narcissistic personality disorder population also includes the people with psychological issues and anti-social personality issues. She gives an estimate that at least 12.6 million people are suffering from narcissistic personality disorder with no conscience. It means that the 12.6 million people have no moral values to judge themselves. They comply with what they are feeling, without thinking about the right and wrong.

More than 60.8 million people are adversely affected in the United States by the narcissistic behavior of the narcissistic parent, narcissistic spouse, narcissistic friend or any other narcissistic family member. Furthermore, she makes a clear statement that the 60.8 million people is just a rough estimate as it does not include the children who are secretively being affected by the narcissistic behavior of their parents. Maternal and paternal narcissism is very common in United States.

According to the DSM-5, prevalence of the

narcissistic personality disorder in the population of United States is 6% while the prevalence of the anti-social symptoms in the personality is as high as 3.3%.

According to this data, there are more than 326 million in the United States (the population is ever-increasing) and the 6% of the total United States population is suffering from narcissistic personality disorder. This means that approximately, 19,560,000 people are suffering from the narcissistic personality disorder. So, if we combine the population is suffering from the narcissistic personality disorder and the population suffering from anti-social personality disorder. Approximately 697,500,000 people lack empathy or have no conscience. As estimated by Brown, these people affect almost 80.8 million people.

Moreover, the DSM-5 proceeds to inform us that almost 50-75% of all the narcissistic patients are men. The remaining narcissistic patients are women and teenage kids.

International Statistics on Narcissistic Personality Disorder

Globally, the DSM-5 states that almost 6.2% of the total world population suffers from the narcissistic personality disorder. Narcissistic personality disorder is recognized outside the United States just like in United States. However, the ICD-10 lists 8 faces of narcissistic personality disorder globally.

Narcissistic personality disorder should not be considered lightly as a high unknown percentile of children and adults from around the globe are suffering from the bad effects of maternal narcissism and paternal narcissism. However, despite having narcissistic issues, many mothers and fathers are seeking help from the professional psychologists so that they can raise their children in a safe, protective and a healthy environment.

Maternal narcissism symptoms

Narcissism is a common human practice of feeling important, needing admiration, attention from others, desiring success and love. To an extent, this is quite normal and in most of the situation, it is being considered as an important personality trait which every person must possess but only until it is occasional and mild. It is because it is perfectly fine to be Narcissist to the extent which could not be classed as a disorder.

However, on the other hand, if there is a person who is characterized by Narcissism quite strongly, or the Narcissist personality traits have gone to an extreme in someone, then this is a personality disorder and it will become highly important to pay attention to its treatment. It is because in such situations Narcissism will have the ability to cause functional impairment and distress and even the situation can last for a longer period of time with ease.

If a person possesses a pattern of abnormal behavior for a longer period of time which are particularly characterized by the feeling of self-importance, lack of empathy and excess need for self-admiration. His constant behavior of seeking excess attention and constant admiration can frustrate other people who are in a relationship with the sufferer of this disorder.

Well, to get a better idea about Narcissistic personality disorder it is important to have a look at its basics to get a better idea about the things. Knowing this will surely help you to understand more facts in an effective way with ease.

Narcissistic personality disorder

A narcissistic personality disorder is one of many other personality disorders. It is a mental sense of suffering from an exaggerated sense self-admiration, self-importance, deep urge of extreme attention, etc.

51

Such people who are suffering from this may have trouble with their relationship because they also have a lack of sympathy and compassion for others.

Such people always feel that they are superior or better than the others who are around them and therefore, they should be treated in special manners accordingly. Well, the fact which remains behind this extreme situation are, this excess confidence is just a mask. Actually, these people have flimsy self-esteem which is vulnerable to even the slightest criticism.

Narcissistic personality disorder can be best defined as a paradox. It is because such people who are suffering from this may act confident and superior but they are lacking at self-esteem and are not actually confident about themselves. They are just craving to seek attention from others and want everyone to praise them only.

Due to their superior attitude, most of the Narcissistic personality disorder sufferers are unable to build positive relationships with others. The Narcissistic personality disorder can become a cause of great disaster not only for the person who is suffering from this but also for the people who are living around that person. These affected persons more often spend much time thinking about themselves only. They often think about the ways to achieve power and success or about the ways to improve their appearance. They try to take advantage of the people who are around them most of the time. The abnormal behavior in most of the people normally begins early in their adulthood or occurs across a different variety of social situations such as in relationships or work life.

Most commonly people who are suffering from this problem are being characterized as self-centered, arrogant, demanding and manipulative. Most of them may also have some sort of splendid illusions or fantasies or could be convinced that they need to have special treatments. In some cases, these people also try to associate themselves with the people they think are unique or have some special capabilities.

It means such people want to be linked with the ones who have been gifted in some way and this is also only for the enhancement of their own self-esteem not to praise the next person. Such people tend to seek excessive attention and admiration and have difficulty when it comes to bear any kind of criticism or defeat.

Fast facts:

Here are some facts about Narcissism which you must know:

• Narcissism is a term which has been come from a particular character named as Narcissus in Greek Mythology.

• Narcissism is being characterized by an extreme sense of self-admiration and self-worth. Features of being prone to irritation, quick to anger and vulnerable to criticism are also associated with this situation.

• For its diagnosis, symptoms or signs of Narcissism must be chronic and persistent.

Causes of Narcissism

Well, the exact cause behind the Narcissism is yet unknown because there are different theories about the cause behind Narcissism. Some people think it is a mix of the things which can be ranged from how a person has been raised or how he or she handled different stressing situations.

However, most of the experts tend to apply a biopsychosocial model for this which means that a combination of social, neurobiological, genetic and environmental factors may have played their roles in formulating a Narcissistic personality.

There is also some evidence that this personality

disorder can be heritable individuals are likely to develop Narcissism disorder if they have any family history of this disorder. However, in some cases, a specific gene interaction can also contribute to the development of Narcissism personality disorder.

While on the other hand, social and environmental factors are also having a prominent influence on the development of Narcissism disorder. In some cases, Narcissism could develop a weakened attachment with their parents or primary caregivers. This can cause a sense of unconnected and unimportant to others in a child. In some cases, the child may tend to believe that he has some defects in his personality which are making him devalued or unwanted. However, permissive parenting such as over-controlling or insensitive behavior can also play an important role in influencing Narcissism disorder.

Although to find out the exact cause of this personality disorder is complex to figure out but, the children who have been raised by a Narcissist are more likely to develop Narcissism disorder. Although parental narcissism can affect the children but even with few maternal narcissistic traits has the ability to affect their daughters in deceptive ways.

Well, if you are new to the realization of a maternal narcissism then you need to keep learning about what you have to deal with. One of the worst things which you may come to know is the fact that your narcissist mother will never change until she finds a way to bring healthier change in her life.

Well to know what signs and symptoms of maternal narcissism can be and how it can affect you, it is highly important to learn about this in a proper way. Well, here we have brought major and most common symptoms of maternal narcissism which are surely going to be better for you to know in this regard.

Maternal Narcissism

A narcissist mother is an arrogant, self-centered and self-involved mother who just loves her own image. She can't tear herself away from the good reflection of her and ultimately her self-love will lead her to the maternal narcissism, a disorder. Narcissism is actually a spectrum disorder, which has been described as a personality disorder and can be classified on the basis of some important personality traits.

There could be only a few things which can be worse as compared to dealing with the mother who is suffering from a narcissist personality disorder. When a kid has a mother, who can never see outside of her own self or her selfish needs, then more often the kids end up by being a punching bag, a slave to every whim of his mother or a servant only. Well, the most important fact to mention here is the mothers suffering from a narcissist personality disorder do not suffer as often as their children do.

Maternal Narcissism Symptoms

Maternal narcissism is being defined as having a mother who is a sufferer of narcissistic personality disorder. Narcissism is a touch of her own feelings which she often tries to project on others and specifically on their children too. Such females are not capable of any empathy or compassion for others even not for their own kids at all. It is because such mothers are unable to put themselves into your shoes to understand or feel how things might affect you. This may be the reason why a lot of people around the world find a need to overcome their personality disorder.

More often they are hypersensitive to defeat, judgment or criticism. However, they will criticize and judge others on a constant basis. When a narcissist mom comes back to the home she always has a demand for consistent attention and admiration. But if you are going to show your back, then it will become a cause to irritate them.

As a result, she would become offensive and attacks you. She is constantly irritated, she is tired because she wants the things in her own way and wants to align your feelings with hers. She always taunts you to be ungrateful for the favors she has given to you as a mother. Even if you fight with her to let her understand the things as you want, she will fight back with you just to win but never to understand the situation.

Although most of the normal parents get into the struggle with their kids to understand them but a narcissist parent only struggles to win from kids. Well, this is truly scary and desperate. It is because every one of us wants to be around a happy mom, always hoping that our mothers will in a good mood and not concerned to generate a rage attack.

Well, for better understanding, here are some characteristics, traits or symptoms of a narcissistic mother which you must understand to know the things in a more effective way. So, have a look at the following maternal narcissism symptoms:

1. She thinks she is always a winner but in public only

Establishing an ideal world-class and successful career, owning your dream home and a perfect family are the things which are never going to be a simple walk in the park. Therefore, no one ever said that this was easier but you always have someone in your life who helps you to make it look that way and yes, she is your mother.

A mother is a woman, everyone admires. She can be a doctor, lawyer, teacher or a judge. She could be the power behind your church and a PTA. More often she balances by contributing to the community which can leave the people in awe while being nimble socially and in their eyes, she is a super-lady.

While most of the people did not know that this super lady has a secret in her life or she has a flaw just

61

like everyone else in this world. No one is the personification of perfection and in this mother's case, this is narcissism. Although the outside world is always embracing her but only you know the fact that your mother is self-centered, easily angered, "always right" and brittle.

A narcissistic mother is more engaged with socialism. She may be a perfect person for her colleagues, friends or relatives but they do not know the person inside her that you know. You may also get a maternal love from your mother but now and then. The reason is that it is always unpredictable and has been punctuated by anger, control and a need which is only to walk on the eggshells.

Narcissistic mothers are more socially engaged and they love to become controlling mothers at their house. She is no longer a female that is wearing a lasting smile which never fades, at least in the eyes of everyone else. She is more demanding, criticizes and will tell you often that you are not up to her standards. Even she never hesitates to degrade you.

2. She will let you feel like a failure

A narcissistic mother is comparatively good at manipulating specifically when the emotions of her kids are involved in the situation. A narcissistic mother always temples to her entire family to address her own desires without giving a thought about what anyone else may need at a specific time. Even if you are not able to fulfill her desires or to let her understand that her needs are more important as compared to anyone else then it is important for you to be prepared for an unwanted and unreal criticism, an attack or defeat.

Even if you are looking for any type of validation then you may have to wait for a longer period of time. In some cases, she will make you feel like you are a total failure when you are not going to do something which she wants you to do right now.

Even the kids who are nurturing under such kind of situation always push themselves back so that no one could ever perceive them in this way. Such kids are unable to define what they want because they never have seen how to express this in front of others. As a result, they are unable to say "what I need or I have some needs" or "I matter."

3. A narcissistic mother gets offended with ease

Normally mothers do a lot of things for their kids but they never let their kids realize that at every step of their lives. However, when it comes to a narcissistic mother, she always has a claim that she has done so much for you in her life. Even if you are not going to give her compliments or appreciation that she wants from you in return she will get upset. Even she will believe that you do not love her.

If you do, then you must do what she actually wanted. Even in some cases, she will start to accuse you of taking her as granted. Because she thinks that you are not appreciating the things she is doing for you as a mother. Even more, she will compare you with the kids of others who she thinks are good with their mother.

4. She is privately opinionated

Well, this is an obvious symptom which you can find almost in every narcissistic mother. A narcissistic mother is always a kind of blasting person who will try to act cool and calm publicly. Even when you are in public with her she tends to be more forgiving. It is because she wants to maintain a positive image of herself in front of the world; even if she is in front of people she does not like much.

To look better in front of people, she will act like she is sweet, caring and cooperative but actually it is not the truth. Moreover, there she will smile to show she is fascinating, she is captivating while having chat with the people she does not even like. It is because she has saved her criticism for home. She loves to do things only when people are seeing her. She will give her opinion privately and would like to describe the things when she will be at her private place.

5. She always looks for faults in you

Whenever you are going to make a fault whether consciously or unconsciously then there is no opportunity for you to get out of the situation by just saying "I am sorry mother." It is because this is never going to be enough for your narcissist mother. More often it becomes harder for you to figure out how to please your mother with your apology and how to let her feel that you are truly ashamed of what you have done.

When you are being accused in your family then the chances would higher that you automatically start to accuse yourself. It will lead you to deep guilt even for the things which are not in your control or beyond your responsibilities. Narcissistic mothers are often expert at projecting or deflecting blame on you. While on the other side, if you are going to make a try to stand for yourself then your narcissistic mother will take it as you attacked her.

6. A narcissistic mother will make you more anxious

A narcissistic mother is never filled with the self-worth or self-confidence. She always wants you to feel inadequate. Even if you are trying hard to do something which deserves appreciation or praise but you will never get any of these in reward.

Well, it is a vital fact that every person needs validation more specifically in the early stages of their life. It is because that is the time which can make someone confident and strong. However, a narcissistic mother may prompt self-doubt in everything which you are going to do and this makes you more nervous and concerned with your doings.

7. Her world only revolves around herself

Normally, kids are the center of attraction for mothers but in case of a narcissistic mother, the only attention of a mother is her own self. It is because she always wanted to be the center of attraction or attention. She needs admiration all the time. A narcissistic mother always waits from you to be adored. She always expects you to praise her and provide her above than all of this. It is because her world is just revolving around her own self and she is unable to see anyone else around except herself.

Narcissistic mothers are unable to understand the feelings or thoughts of others. This is actually one of the most important qualities of nurturing the kids for the parents. However, the mothers who are suffering from narcissism are lacking at it and they always looking for the ways to have constant attention and admiration for themselves.

More often when you are going to discuss something

about your issues with your mother, she always tends the topic towards herself. At the end, the entire talk would be diverted about herself only. Even when you will try to share your feelings or thoughts with your mother she will always try to top your feelings with her own. Instead of listening to you she will make it to talk about herself.

8. Boundaries are not existing in your house

If you are living with a narcissistic mother, then you will feel that either there are no boundaries existing in your place or these are being violated on a consistent basis. It is because narcissistic mother sees others, especially her own children as her extension to manipulate and control. As a golden child for her, she would like to reflect herself through you and wishes to project the same to the world.

As a culprit, this is your duty to take the entire blames of the problems of your family, endure the worst abuse of her, and even handle irrational responsibilities. Either way, your mother will tell you what you should think or feel and will insist you on your obedience with his own version of the reality. No matter how false, harmful or absurd it could be. Although one of the most important and difficult things which most of the people want to do for themselves is to establish healthy and successful boundaries but this is the thing which you will be unable to do with a narcissistic mother.

9. She teaches her daughters that love is never unconditional

A narcissistic mother teaches her daughter that love is always conditional. It will be given only when the daughters behave in accordance with her maternal whims and expectations. As adults, such daughters suffer from difficulty to overcome the feelings of emotional emptiness, inadequacy, sadness, and disappointment. Most of them may also have a fear of rejection from others which will lead them to unhealthy and unsuccessful romantic relationships with their partners. As well as they will likely to develop an unrelenting self-criticism, tendency to perfectionism, frustration or self-sabotage.

10.   A narcissistic mother will live through your life

Almost every mother in the entire world wants her child to get succeeded. However, some narcissistic mothers set expectations from their kids not for the benefit of their kids but for the accomplishment of their own selfish needs and dreams, instead of raising a child with his own emotions, values, thoughts, and goals. As a result, the kids become an extension of personal wishes of their mothers and the individuality of such children often gets diminished.

A narcissistic mother will try some common methods of controlling you just like putting you into guilt trip on a continuous basis just to make you do what she wanted. She will let you realize her sacrifices which resultantly, make you felt indebted to her and you will surely owe the complete obedience. Even more, if you failed to do what she wanted from you, she would withdraw her love quite easily. In such case either you will get a severe punishment or a treatment of her long-lasting silence. This will give you the impression that you will be loved only when you are going to prove your worth to her.

11. Competitive marginalization

Some narcissistic mothers are threatened by the potential, willpower, promise, and success of their offspring as they have the ability to challenge the self-esteem of them. As a result, a narcissistic mother might make an effort to put her children down, so that she could remain superior. This type of competitive marginalization will include unnecessary criticism, unreasonable judgment, nit-picking, unfavorable comparisons, invalidation of positive emotions and behavior, and rejection of accomplishments and success.

The most common theme behind all of these put down methods is "There is always something wrong with your doings or you can never be good enough to compete." With the help of lowering the confidence of her kids, a narcissistic mother will satisfy or boost her own insecure self-worth.

12. Superiority and Grandiosity

Most of the narcissistic mothers have a self-image which is falsely inflated with an arrogant sense about what they do and who they are. More often the people around such people are not being treated humanely, but as tools which can be used for personal gain only.

Similarly, some kids of the narcissistic mothers are also being objectified in a similar manner, while others are being taught to possess the same and forged the superiority complex of "we are better as compared to what they are." However, this sense of impressive entitlement is exclusively based on egotistical, material and superficial trappings which are attained at the expense of the humanity, relatedness, and conscientiousness of someone. One could become superior but by being less human.

13.   A narcissistic mother might be extremely touchy and inflexible

Certain narcissistic mothers become highly inflexible when it comes to the expected behavior of the kids. They start to regulate their kids even on the minor details and often become upset when seeing any deviation in them. Some of the narcissistic mothers also become reactive with ease; however, the reasons behind this irritation may vary from kids to kids and can be ranged from lack of attention and obedience to the shortcomings and faults which they have perceived.

Well, the most common reason behind the inflexibilities of the mothers can be their desire to take control of their children. Narcissistic mothers might respond disproportionally or negatively when they see that the kids will not be pulled by their strings always.

14.   She is having a lack of empathy

The most common manifestation of a narcissistic mother is her inability to be mindful of their own feelings and thoughts of their kids and to validate these as important and real. What she thinks about her kids is the only thing that matters for her. As a result, children who come under this type of maternal influence respond with any of the following three survival instincts over time:

• The kids may stand-up and fight for themselves.

• They may go away and have distance from their family.

• While some of such kids may begin to freeze their own personality. They substitute the invalidated real-self of them with an untrue façade or may end up with adopting the traits of their narcissistic mothers.

15. Dependency and codependency

Some narcissistic mothers have expectations from their children that they will take care of them throughout their lives. This is a common type of financial, physical and emotional dependency. Even there is nothing bad in taking care of the older parents and more often it is being considered as one of the most admirable traits in our society.

But a narcissistic mother normally manipulates her child into making unnecessary sacrifices even with the little regard of the personal needs and priorities of her child. In most of the cases, a narcissistic mother told her child "Do not leave her, I need you, I can't live without you, etc." Resultantly, all of such things make it impossible for you to spend your anonymous life. Even mover, such kind of emotional attitude from a mother can stop a kid to establish his own priorities other than fulfilling the needs of his mother. Even, a narcissistic mother may also maneuver her adult child into codependency.

16. Possessiveness and jealousy

More often a narcissistic mother hopes to dwell her child under her influence on a permanent basis. Therefore, she may become extremely jealous by seeing the independence and growing maturity of her child. If her kid is going to take any perceived act of separation or individuation which can be ranged from making friends which are not approved by her, spending time on his own primacies to choosing an academic course or career which she did not think about he will be interpreted personally or in a negative way.

Particularly, the appearance of a perfect or romantic partner in the life of an adult offspring can also be viewed as a threat. A narcissistic mother frequently respond to such kind of situation with competition, rejection or criticism. It is because in the eyes of a narcissistic mother no interloper or romantic partner could be perfect or good enough for her kids. Even no one can challenge her for dominance of her child.

17.   A narcissistic mother shames her kids chronically

Shaming is one of the most favorite weapon of narcissistic mothers to stop their children from developing sense self-importance or individual identity. She shames her kids to ensure that they could never grow self-reliably or go outside of seeking her approval or validation. Even she will shame her children for not achieving enough socially, personally, academically or professionally.

She will shame children not only for being uncompetitive in their lives but also for the decision of their choices regarding academic majors, career, friends, partner, lifestyle, dress manners, personality, preferences and every other thing in their lives which can come under the inquiry of a narcissistic mother. A narcissistic mother shames her children for acting with every sense of agency which has the ability to threaten her sense of power and control over her kids.

18.   She tries to set up comparisons among her children and their peers

Just like every narcissistic, a narcissistic mother will try to impose a triangulation by building triangles among her children with their friends or peers. In this triangulation, she will compare her kids with their peers in destructive manners and will teach them that they have fallen short in term of their personality, obedience, behavior, looks, or achievements.

Even in some cases, a narcissistic mother also puts two siblings against each other by her unfavorable comparisons. In this race, she may make one of her children as golden one while other a fall guy. This form of child evaluation has the ability to leave a painful imprint on them. Even the children will start to compare others with themselves as a method to evaluate their self-importance.

19. She often competes her kids, disturbs their shift to adulthoods and may cross sexual boundaries

It is more common in narcissistic mothers to compete with their kids, especially with their daughters. In some cases, a narcissistic mother may overvalue her own sex powers and looks. More often female narcissistic view other females as their competition therefore, in case of a narcissistic mother, she may look her own daughter as a threat. Resultantly, she might devalue the physical appearance of her daughter, shame or criticize the personality of her own daughter.

On the other hand, some of the narcissistic mothers may portray their daughters or demand perfection in her physical looks. Even she can expose her to inappropriate discussions about exhibit her body, placing accentuate on the value of her body appearance or even sex. She might teach her children that the women can derive value from their body or capability to please a man physically. Narcissistic mothers with histrionic tendencies may seduce her children's friends to demonstrate the superiority over the younger competition of her.

While in the cultures where sexuality is far away from restrictions, narcissistic mothers may also attempt to choke burgeoning sexuality of their daughters and punish them for being less than abstinent. A narcissistic mother may fail to provide proper education regarding sex or her growing body to her daughters.

20. A narcissistic mother may have an obsession with the external even at the expenses of the needs of her own child

For a narcissistic mother, something that meant to her is only her appearance. She can construct a fake image of being a sweet, loving, charitable or caring person to others while gossiping about all of them or abusing her children physically, emotionally or sexually. She might be enjoying the social status of being a mother while she is not fulfilling any of her maternal responsibilities.

She might show off her kids without even tending to their basic psychological or emotional needs. It is because for a narcissistic mother how things are looking is more important as compared to how they actually are. Sometimes, depending on the social status of a narcissistic mother, she may enlist others to help to care for her children while neglecting to give the attraction or affection to her own children when they are around and may treat them as annoyances rather than as humans. At times she could be enough cold that she refuses to touch her kids altogether.

21. A narcissistic mother may engage her kids in terrible boundary-breaking

In the end, narcissistic mothers may become trapped in covert emotional incest. In such situations, they often make their kids the center of their own world and make them responsible for fulfilling their emotional needs. Rather than being a parent figure for their kids, they will make them feel obligated for the fulfillment of her arbitrary expectations and desires.

She will violate the basic needs of her children and will demand to know every aspect of their lives. She may enter in the rooms of her children without knocking, interrogate them about their friends or partners, read their diaries without asking. She will continuously try to keep her child from growing up whether that means going on date, moving out of the house, becoming aware of adulthood or getting married.

22. A narcissistic mother will emotionally invalidate, gas lights or guilt-trips her children

The reaction of a child to the abuse of her narcissistic mother frequently met with shaming, further gas lighting and invalidation. A narcissistic mother lacks the feeling of empathy even for her own children and often gets failed to consider the basic needs of them.

She is disposed to tell her kids that abused never occurred and it is much common for her to claim that her kids are being overreacting or oversensitive to unbearable psychological violence acts. At the same time, a narcissistic mother will try to manipulate and control her kids with emotional outbursts. Even when her child is expressing her emotions, she will invalidate them entirely. Some of the most common examples of a narcissistic mother include:

- Guilt Trip: "I have done a lot for you but you are always ungrateful for my virtues."

- Blaming: "if I am unhappy, it is entirely your fault."

- Shaming: "your poor grade is always an embarrassment for the entire family."

- Emotional coercion: "you are not a good child unless you are not up to my standard."

- Negative comparison: "why can't you be a better person as your sister."

- Manipulative punishment or rewards: "if you do not pursue the best at the subjects I chose for you, I will not support you anymore."

- Unreasonable pressure: "you have to perform at your best to make me happier."

A narcissistic mother always redirects the focus to her own needs and will guilt trips her kids at even the tiniest sign of perceived disobedience. The most common theme which is running through any form of manipulation is that the love is given to their kids on a conditional basis rather than making that unconditional reward as a natural expression of healthy parenting. Even on the other hand, the love withholding is being used as a punishment or threat for the kids.

Commonly, emotional and empathetical mothers are agreed to the emotional wellbeing of their kids while a narcissistic mother always represents an imitation maternal instinct.

Consequences of having a narcissistic mother

It's a natural human feeling to desire a mother who loves everything about you. It is normal to put your head on your mother's chest and feel her love and sympathy. We always need and look for the unconditional love of a trusted mother. Motherhood is always idealized making it always hard for the children of narcissistic mothers from facing their past. It is difficult for most people to imagine or be unable to love and care for their children, and no children certainly don't want to believe because of her mother.

Narcissistic mothers are emotionally damaged personalities and are multi-generational, which means that they are transmitted from generation to generation. When a mother suffers a narcissistic injury, he will leave her children unless he takes the time to heal her childhood wounds before she becomes a mother. Children of a narcissistic mother suffer greatly as they become the narcissistic representation of the maternal personality rather than mothers who satisfy their emotional needs. Children are ready to respond to their needs by creating a reverse emotional flow.

Impact of living with a narcissistic personality

Living with a narcissist person means that you will be strongly influenced, whether in an intimate relationship, in a work environment or in a family situation. They will try to dominate and control your life to the point where they will become the goal of your life. They usually use mind control techniques against you to become the kind of person they want you to be. Basically, you become a person who is waiting for you with your hands and feet, putting your desires and needs in the foreground.

You will be humiliated, criticized, shouted, judged, ridiculed, ridiculed, treated with contempt and controlled by someone you think you love and that you can really love. You will not be allowed to obtain your opinions or ideas and, in general, you should ask permission to do a lot of things. You seem to be making your own decisions, but these are the tricks of these manipulators. You must do the things that suit you at all costs.

You mostly have low self-esteem especially around them. You may feel dependent on them or think that you cannot imagine life without them. This makes it very difficult to get out of the situation, but leaving it is usually the best option available to you. You may need to learn more about narcissists, anger, abuse and how to control yourself in order to perceive the damage caused by their decision to leave or simply to run and prepare. Living with a narcissist personality or being raised by a narcissistic mother has important consequences on you, so it's important to understand the consequences and take the right steps.

Do not confuse narcissistic personality disorder, self-confidence, and self-esteem. Those who enjoy high self-esteem remain humble. If you live with a narcissistic personality disorder, you risk being selfish, boasting and ignoring the feelings and needs of others. It was previously thought that people with narcissistic personality disorder had a high degree of confidence in their self-esteem, but in their depths they were unsafe. This theory was supported by the defensive state in which these individuals enter when they are provoked. Recent research ignores the previous theory and now suggests that if you suffer from a narcissistic personality disorder, you are also likely to have great confidence in yourself on the surface and below the surface.

If you live with a narcissistic personality disorder, it will probably affect your daily life in a negative way. In general, you may feel unsatisfied with life in general and disappointed when you do not like others or do not give yourself special treatment or attention.

However, it is likely that your business, your personal relationships, and your social relationships are growing; you cannot see your role in these events. People with narcissistic personality disorder are unable to perceive the harmful effects that their behavior causes on themselves and others. If you are being raised by a person having this disorder, people may not appreciate your closeness and dissatisfaction at work, at home or in your social life.

What happens when you are being raised by a narcissistic mother?

When you are being raised by a narcissistic mother,

you grow up and think that you are not good enough. You are diligent and happy, affectionate and gentle. You never deviate from what your parents expect in school, with friends, in every aspect of life. When you have a narcissistic mother, you cannot understand why you are not good enough. Why do you scream when you learn that you have done nothing wrong?

Your classmates go to the party, concert and more. However, you are very well sent to your room immediately after dinner as it is served. When you grow up with a narcissistic mother, you realize that you should not hide your notes about your younger siblings; you have to hide them from your mother. You see that your mother gets angry because you are not informing that you are going to the party for some reasons.

However, although the effects of being raised by the narcissistic mother are permanent, it is possible to manage the anxiety that arises from this experience. Aging with a narcissistic mother can have a profound effect on you and might lead to not trust yourself. When you are being raised by a mother that ignores your feelings, you will be confused as an adult.

In general, children become an extension of their mother's personality by becoming their mini version and responding to the needs of beauty, success and other wishes of their mothers. The consequences of this dysfunctional dynamic can make co-dependent children and do not become healthy and independent adults. Being co-dependent on their mother, their world revolves around their mothers and frustrates separatism and individualism.

Other negative effects of this unhealthy dynamic include low self-esteem, inability to establish healthy relationships, a sense of entitlement, the need for perfection, and a shift to intense self-criticism. These children lose their energy and are often punished or dismissed when they do not meet the needs and wishes of their mothers.

If you are wondering what actually happens to your personality development when you are being raised by narcissistic mother, here are some of the consequences and characteristics of having a narcissistic mother. Let's have a look at these consequences

- **Chronic self-blame**

Narcissistic parents may or may not be abusive publicly, yet they are almost emotionally deaf or very concerned about their own fear of hearing our pain. Because emotionally sensitive children who yearn for love cannot just get out of the house and find a new family, they often inspire hope by sacrificing self-respect. They think that they are the problem and if they are calmer, or happier, their mother will not yell, ignore or criticize them all the time.

• Terrified of their needs

Narcissistic parents can terrify the children of their needs. They may be buzzing for a moment, and they do not seem to need anything from their classmates or their friends. Then the crisis breaks out and suddenly, in a way that bothers them a lot, always calls their friends or seeks constant comfort. The quickest way to eliminate the need, after all, is to satisfy it immediately, people who fear the most tend to want to be afraid of their needs and seem needy.

- **Parentified child**

Sensitive teens can develop a laser-like approach to meet the needs of their parents. They organize their lives according to the happiness of others, convinced of the need to strengthen the respect of their parents or to avoid their next explosion by paying special attention to their every whim or desire. A child who is afraid of becoming a small adult often grows up to constantly worry about selfishness. They can hate their own needs and see them as a burden to others.

- **Absence of boundaries**

Because of the lack of boundaries, narcissistic mothers tend to view their daughters as threats and attachments to their vanity. Through advice and criticism, they try to turn their daughter into a copy of themselves or their flawless self. At the same time,

96

they do not expose their daughter to unwanted and self-defeating aspects, such as egocentrism, stubbornness, selfishness, and coldness, but also unpleasant traits for their mothers.

• Narcissistic abuse

Narcissistic abuse includes repeated shame and control; undermine the development of the girl's identity, creating low self-esteem and insecurity. They can't trust their own feelings and motives and concludes that it is his fault to hate his mother, without realizing that their mother will never be satisfied. In severe cases of physical or emotional abuse or neglect, children of a narcissistic mother may feel that they do not have the right to exist; they are a burden to their mother and must never be born. Some mothers lie and hide the abuse. Children do not learn to protect and defend themselves. You may feel helpless or do not recognize the violence later in an abusive relationship with an adult.

• Lack of emotional availability

The emotional comfort and closeness offered by the mother's tenderness and natural care are absent. Narcissistic mothers can take care of their material needs, but they give up emotionally. The children do not realize what is missing, but they long for their mother's tenderness and understand that they can experience with relatives, friends or other relationships between mothers and children. You can look for other relationships but often have an emotional style.

• You blame yourself constantly

Narcissistic parents may or may not be abusive publicly, but they are almost certainly emotionally deaf, very concerned about their own fear of hearing our pain. Because emotionally sensitive children who yearn for love cannot just get out of the house and find a new family, they often inspire hope by sacrificing self-respect. They often accuse themselves of keeping some hope in their lives.

• Suffer from narcissism in other relationships

If you are sympathetic or sensitive to your nature, you are likely to react to echoism, named after the Echo siren, who curses for repeating the last words heard. Just as the Narcissists love their reflection, echo loves the Narcissus. The narcissistic mother who burst without collapse or warning whenever a child dares to express their need to force sensitive children to occupy as little space as possible as if all expectations were selfish. Like echoes, ecologists have a hard time making them heard and often find themselves with exceptionally narcissistic partners.

• Become a pleasure for people

Teenagers can develop an approach to meet the needs of their parents. They organize their lives according to the happiness of others. Basically, they become a pleasure for the people. They want to do everything keeping in mind the happiness of others and control their desire so they cannot be a cause of any problem in the future. To recover from childhood, we must first be able to determine how our actions have shaped the treatment we have been given; you cannot do something to heal the wound you are unable to see.

It is common for the children of a narcissistic mother to become a pleasure for people. This is because when a child of the mother whose main concern is pain and unresolved problems, the child is entangled. The child often wonders about the error that his/her mother has often upset. He/she will believe that if he extends to his/her mother, he will receive the love for which he/she aspires.

• Impaired emotional intelligence

Often, these children's separate themselves from their own thoughts and feelings as they try to win their mother's passion so that they cannot identify and label their feelings. More literally than otherwise, they tend to be out of sight.

• Lack of true self-esteem

Often, children of narcissistic parents are raised feeling not well fed in everything they do. This is because they were corrected at an early age and told that they were always doing bad things. The narcissistic mother is never happy with the way others do things. While the beloved mother conveys the message of love, narcissistic mother concerned only validates the accomplishments that make her look good. As this type of validation is just a false and false version of true love, the children tend to confuse themselves as an adult, seeking to establish relationships that work in this familiar way. Look at others so that they feel good and do not be surprised when this does not happen regularly.

• Very rejection sensitive

Narcissistic Mother makes you learn that you will one day be a part of the Mom team so you can enjoy the sun while you can be dropped the next day if you hate or disappoints her. Children of narcissistic mother enter adolescence still seeking to validate with friends and romantic partners, but it is also very interactive and explores the horizon in search of potential problems and rejection.

• Attracts those with high narcissistic characteristics

We all tend to be fashionable and attractive to us, and this includes sadly an unpopular girl raised by a sharing mother who can be attracted to those who treat her like her mother and show them the same qualities. The unconditional love of the parent and the inability to deal with the terrible truth that your parents don't like you are what makes the child at hand and allows the narcissistic mother to continue hurting him/her as soon as he/she becomes an adult instead of trying to get out of this situation.

• **Anxiety, addiction, depression or panic attacks**

Because there is no special meaning in the son of narcissistic adults, adults often wonder what they want to do in life. Is it okay to say this or that? Is it permissible to feel this way? This insecurity becomes heavy with time. An adult child cannot trust even themselves, so it will be difficult to trust others. In relationships, the adult child will not know how to express his needs and feelings. Because of this frustration, you may resort to drinking, eating, obsession or panic to cope with the situation.

- **The difficulty of establishing healthy relationships**

The children of a narcissistic mother are afraid of being abandoned or rejected by the person they love. Although we are all afraid at a certain level, our partner shares many good things with us, but children of narcissists are always terrified of saying or making a mistake. They believe that if they make a mistake, their partners or friends will leave them.

In the end, the narcissistic mother will see herself as a whole being and her child as partial beings formed by a small part of themselves. Her way of treating the child is a true reflection of how she feels to be treated. The children must serve, obey and respect all the whims of the narcissistic father to make up for the part they have lost. In the minds of narcissistic parents, it is the only purpose of the child in life and its use is the same as eating healthy and exercising: you just take care of yourself.

Such as diet and exercise, children should be monitored until they feel well. The narcissistic mother thinks her mother serves her children by babysitting them. The grandparents will be proud and will appreciate the narcissistic mother for something big. They brought this wonderful child to the world that is so happy to attribute everything to his impressive abilities as parents.

Doctors say that if you cannot fight your mother while you grow up, you will choose to be like them. Why because it's the easiest and most convenient option. To live in a violent environment, the child must be similar to those around him. Is it like a defense mechanism? We will imitate the narcissistic mother and we will often find ourselves manipulating or repressing others. If we do not question our actions and ask for help, we can develop a type of unhealthy narcissism that could harm our environment. There are people who manipulate others to get what they want. They ask for approval and rely on the need for confidentiality. These people like to provoke negative reactions in others and use them to meet their needs.

In general, the narcissistic adult child will ignore his needs in his relationships with his friends and other important people. It's an automatic and unconscious behavior to put everyone in the first place. In the recovery phase, you must learn to recognize your needs and take into account bilateral relations. Everyone should have the chance to express themselves without any judgment.

Signs that you have a narcissistic mother

The relationship between mother and child is so fundamental that it is tragic to have a mother in front of one's own life. Mother's love is closest to most people for unconditional consideration, and it's often the safety net that allows us to go out and face the world, knowing that we can go back no matter what difficulty of our experience. . We often want to get rid of that extreme respect in old age, and that luxury has always been someone's foundation. The absence of this fundamental stability in your life can be a disaster for life, but the main point of healing is total awareness and acceptance of the relationship reality.

When our basic experience of love is very detrimental, it is difficult to establish future relationships based on trust and dependency. Perhaps we have fear as well as self-protection that can create a distance from our partners and we end up repeating patterns that we hate in our fathers. This is the actual tragedy; however, it does not have to be an inevitable result: once we realize it, we have the ability to prevent it from becoming a model for generations at a time. However, it can take a lot of courage and support.

Your mother must accept and see who she is: a very sad person no longer has the ability to harm her unless she is granted. She deprived herself of the best of her life: a lifelong love for a child throughout her life. It's not up to you to organize this for her, and her energy needs to be reserved for her own needs. Your challenge will be to consider yourself worthy and worthy of love, and to risk really relying on another person. You will have to put aside the emotional obstacles while relying on your intelligence to know who deserves the risk. This can happen in friendships and in basic relationships. Here are some of the signs of a narcissistic mother.

Her standards are extremely high

Those who have the NDP often have high standards for others. It may extend to their children and involve thinking that their child is the best and deserves to be recognized or considered an extension. Narcissists also think that their child must be a star of his/her career or be very handsome, beyond the reasonable level. This is already a problem when it affects other people, for example, a parent who has a relationship with a child's teacher or teachers, which create more problems for the child, which can be perceived in a more negative way.

She ends up being the victim

Narcissism can be a stressful experience because they always find a way to become a victim. You may realize that your mother is still complaining about her misunderstanding. The narcissistic mother can also find a way to feel hurt, even if the problem is not related to her.

She really believes that you are perfect

All parents believe that their children are perfect, but the narcissistic mother takes it to the extreme. Another common feature of narcissistic parents is to display their narcissism about their children as ideals or special, with blame. The narcissistic mother can explain any negative comment because to try to get out of the feeling of jealousy.

She doesn't seem to care about what's going on in your life

Most of the parents often tell their children everything that goes on in their life without asking you what's going on in your life. Or do they just tell you to put a happy face, even if you really feel it? If you find yourself grasping your feelings under a carpet, it may indicate that you have a narcissistic mother. A narcissistic mother is very interested in her own needs. We often think that the ideal mother is the one who puts the needs of the children first, but a person who lacks empathy and perspective may face more difficulties because she may have difficulty understanding the needs of the children's.

Sometimes you feel you are the mother

If you act as a caregiver rather than a child because

you are young, this is just one way your parents can benefit. Other ways may include borrowing money without paying. Sometimes a mother does something good to her son/ daughter, for example by praising him, congratulating him or helping him with housework, but she expects her children to give him this favor with a lot of help and praise.

She expects worship

A dominant mother often needs a lot of attention and praise. She expects you to follow or respect everything she says without any question from others. They can attack children or other family members if they do not get what they consider to be enough attention or praise.

She is very nice but not all the time

What happens to narcissists mothers is that they are incredibly cute and often do what they can to win the interests of all. But it did not last long. If people seem to be attracted to their mother and are very appreciated from the first impression, the fact that their interaction with others becomes a bad experience over time.

She cares a lot about what others think

Although it is good to want beautiful things, it is likely that your mother will carry them to the limit. Narcissists like to show their high reputation and emphasize their status. If your mother shows new purchases or brags a lot, she can be narcissistic.

She cannot take criticism

Narcissists are good at criticizing others, but they have trouble seeing any problem in themselves. They are also very poor to receive criticism and get angry when they suggest it's not perfect. Most people do not like criticism but the narcissists are so sensitive. A narcissistic mother may cry or scream or rage whenever she is criticized and feels she has been criticized.

She seeks for attention at all times

Most people like to attract attention, but narcissistic mothers want it. They think that the world revolves around them and will not deal with it well when they are not getting the attention. They always want to be in limelight. Traditionally, mothers are supposed to love understanding, love, and passion. So it can really get worse when your needs do not seem to fit someone else's needs.

She is mixed in all types of misunderstandings

Because narcissist's mothers believe that the world should revolve around them, it can lead to many misunderstandings. Mothers like this struggle with their relationships because they find it difficult to communicate with others. They're fine as long as they focus on them, but they often discuss misunderstandings assuming everything they say or do is related to them.

Get hurt when you don't involve her

When making important decisions, such as changing jobs or getting married, she wants herself to be involved. The narcissist mother acts in such a way as to protect him and if they believe that a decision has been made without her involvement, she cannot control it. She can become cruel, guilty, and defensive and offer huge amounts of shame and guilt to the other.

She rejects the people that challenge her

If you challenge someone who clearly says you do not like it or respect it, you reject them as well as dislike them internally. It is because of the fact being narcissistic, you cannot tolerate anyone who rejects your opinion or challenges you.

She doesn't want you to win

Examine your story together and see if your mother tried to win in any case. This behavior can range from wanting to look younger or more attractive than a girl, from flirting with a romantic partner or a woman to a child, from competing with a child in commercial success and the list goes on and on.

She ignored your needs over the years

Narcissistic mother feelings can be easily hurt, so notice if your mother feels ridiculed all the time and for the smallest things. They are easily offended. Whatever you do for her, it will not be enough. Because narcissists concentrate on themselves, they often find it difficult to give the time to others. Narcissistic mother ignores you as a child and always put herself first. As a result, when you are an adult, you may have trouble connecting to the phone with your mother, not listening, or letting you talk during your visit. In any case, there is certainly a tendency to abandon.

Tips to heal yourself if you are raised by a narcissistic mother

If you have been raised by Narcissus, there are some things to consider. First, ask for treatment or advice. It will help you to find out what the world really is, how relationships should work, what mature and healthy love is, how to calm down and create better opportunities for yourself.

Second, do your research. The more you read and talked about narcissism with others, the more the subject will become clear. If you face the psychological consequences of narcissistic parenting, remember that you are not alone. The beauty of borders is to recognize what you want and do not want, and how you are willing to treat it and not treat it. Setting limits can cause a lot of anxiety for women whose mothers are narcissistic, especially when they set these limits to their mothers.

Here are the tips to heal yourself if you are raised by a narcissistic mother

Determine what you want

This step may be easier than doing, because putting the needs of others in front of you may be your default setting. Maybe you want to go shopping for or you may want to write what you felt and what you wanted. This will help children of narcissistic mothers to identify what they felt and wanted was reasonable and understandable.

Determine the emotions that come when you determine what you want

The central feelings of women whose parents are narcissistic are often guilt, anger, and shame. Remember, it does not matter how you feel as the feelings pass. For most of the people, moments of happiness feels like fleeting while negative moments feel endless. When negative feelings appear, notice this where you feel it in your body. Then let the negative emotions flow, using an image that suits you.

Decide what the limit is

It is difficult to experiment with new behaviors, especially those that concern us. It may be helpful to keep in mind that anxiety is a very sensitive and predictable process. Something terrible will happen. Even worse, we certainly do not have the ability to handle this terrible thing.

The goal is to change your relationship with anxiety. The relationship is no longer a relationship with a winner and a loser. Instead, when you accept your feelings and know what you want, anxiety becomes a problem that you can face.

What is the right approach to heal yourself from a narcissistic mother?

People suffering from a narcissistic disorder must be loved as well as accepted all the time. When they do not get what they want emotionally, they will go to a place where they have to reject those who provoked their disobedience, even if they are small or insignificant. If they receive a critical or unpleasant comment on LinkedIn or Facebook, they will be too angry about the challenge and will do their best to prove that the competitor is wrong.

Keep in mind that you do not need any therapeutic training, to begin with, and what you see if you have a narcissistic sore that needs healing. You have to give a shut-up call to all the noise and all the conversations, get into what you feel deeply and be brave enough to allow yourself to feel the weight of your emotions. If it is scary or overwhelming, look for a good therapist that supports you. Once you understand what makes you uncomfortable and unacceptable, you can explore the root of the problem.

Knowing how to treat a narcissistic mother and healing from this information are two different problems. Lack of self-confidence, reduced abuse, obsessive thinking, excessive anxiety, increased survival instinct and fear responses are common among narcissistic adult children. The partial perception of reality imposed by the narcissistic mother on the child has serious consequences for adults at work and at home. In attacking the effects of narcissism, one finds satisfaction. Here are the important steps:

Recognition

The first step in the recovery process is to recognize that there is anything wrong in the parents' behavior. Nobody can recover from something they refuse to admit. Most of the narcissistic parents choose the favorite child who behaves as if they are walking on water. The important thing to keep in mind is that narcissistic mothers see their child as their extension. They take the credit of their children successes while rejects the failure.

Study

Once you have recognized narcissism, it is necessary to get an education about the disorder and its impact on the family system as a whole. Narcissism is partial biology as other members of the family may also suffer from the disorder and environmental behavior such as trauma, shame, abuse, and neglect may be narcissistic and part the choice as a teenager, identity and acceptability. Since there may be narcissistic disorders or personality in the family, it is easy to follow the pattern. Environmental and selection factors can increase the narcissistic behavior in children that has been strengthened in 18 years.

Recount

This next step is convenient at first but becomes more difficult with the resulting narcissistic effect. For each sign of narcissistic symptoms, remember several examples in childhood and when the behavior is obvious. The more you go through this step, the more healing effect will be important. Every memory must be rewritten with a new dialogue like My parents are narcissistic and they treat me like that. It's completely different from the previous internal dialogue that I'm not good enough.

Recognize

Amid the previous stage, negligence of the narcissistic mother is very likely to become apparent. It can be abused by the child physically; aggression, restraint, mental; silent therapy, light gas, verbal; angry, interrogative, emotional as well as sexual; abuse and humiliation. Not all events need trauma therapy, but some may require repetition and severity.

Grief

The grieving process has five stages: denial, anger, negotiation, depression and finally acceptance. Most of the people trouble believing at first that their mother narcissism had affected them and that it was a denial. As glorious as the image of his narcissistic mother was, it was a depression. The other parent is sometimes expected to be angry at not adequately protecting his children from trauma. Or are absorbed to not be realized or met before. It is important to go through all stages of the pain to be accepted.

Grow

It's a good place to go back and have a better perspective. Start by thinking about how the deformed image of the narcissistic mother in the world and in the human being is the current belief. Then go to the promises made internally as a result. Fight distorted images or promises from the point of view of newly acquired reality. Continue this process until a new perspective is formed and is now part of the ongoing internal dialogue. This fundamental step frees the person from narcissistic lies and false facts.

Forgive

You cannot change the past; you can only understand what happens. When tolerance is real, it has a strong conversion effect. Remember that forgiveness is not for the offender, it is for the forgiver. It is better to forgive faithfully in small portions at a time than to forgive the public. This allows the execution of other offenses in the future or in the past. Do not impose this step, do it at a comfortable pace for the benefits to last a lifetime.

Once these steps were completed, it will be easier for you to deal with yourself as well as to identify other narcissists at work, in society or even in your home. Moreover, now narcissistic behavior will no longer increase your anxiety, frustration or depression.

Grief stages for adult children of narcissistic parents

Here are the stages of grief for adult children of narcissistic parents

Acceptance: First, we must accept that the mother has a limited empathy and love; otherwise we cannot stop denying our feelings and our learning. Acceptance is the first step in recovery once you understand the problem.

Denial: When we were kids, we had to deny that our parents could not love or sympathize for their survival. Baby craves for love above anything else; we need denial to continue our growth and to survive.

Negotiation: We have been negotiating with the narcissistic mother all the way through our lives, internally and with them. We looked forward to changing, which will be different the next time we need it. We have tried many things over the years to win their love and approval.

Anger: We are very angry when we came to know that our emotional needs have not been satisfied and that this has had a major and negative impact on our lives. We are angry at parents and against ourselves for allowing models to evolve and hang on.

Depression: We are very sad to neglect the hope and vision of the kind of mother we wanted. We realize they will never be as loving as we would like. We feel like orphans or children without parents. We abandon all expectations. We regret the loss of seeing these expectations.

During the grieving process, you will come back at every step. Do not continue to heal until you firmly accept that your narcissistic mother has these limitations. Only then can you grief properly. If you do not agree, come back and work again. This is the basic condition for the next action. Wait for guilt to lift the ugly head. You work through a major cultural

129

taboo to hold this work. Record your feelings, talk to your favorite people and to your loved ones and most importantly take care of yourself when you treat them with sadness and acceptance. Be courageous in your healing and look for others who want to join your team.

It is really important to embrace acceptance by letting emotions emerge. If enough time has been processed, you will clear the shock. This does not mean that there will be no scars or that they will completely overcome the trauma of childhood. But with recovery, you feel better and your coping skills improve. Scars are proof that you are working completely. By absorbing the losses, you will feel like melting the ice, but you will eventually become a nice and wise person.

If you think you are dealing with a narcissistic mother, be sure to consult a therapist for help.

As a daughter of a narcissistic mother, you feel shame and think of this as your fault. Shame makes you doubt yourself. Curled in an ocean of doubt, you cannot see these movements as they are a desperate attempt to support the mother at your expense. Revealing these movements and naming them properly them is the first step towards healing.

Raised by a Narcissist? 8 Healing Things to Do for Yourself

Narcissism operates in a range from healthy to malicious narcissism, with many intermediate degrees. Many people may have one or two narcissistic features without being narcissistic. When you get absorbed and always place yourself before others, it can be a sign of narcissism. Narcissistic tendencies are found everywhere. However, the difference is that some people have more signs and attributes than others.

The general definition of narcissism is the person who has excessive admiration for herself and for the person who generally cares most about herself. To help you better understand narcissism; consider the symptoms you may encounter when dealing with a narcissist as they can help you to deal effectively with a narcissist. Consider the symptoms of the narcissist and find out if you can identify them in this person. Once you know what makes them narcissist, you can learn to manage them in a positive way.

Healthy narcissism is fundamentally self-esteem. You believe in yourself and what you can do, and your self-assessment is realistic. You can empathize with others and understand their feelings and perspectives. You are not destroyed by criticisms, mistakes or failures. Your own feelings can withstand the rise and fall of life and the opinions of people. On the other hand, malignant narcissists have a very fragile feeling and reaction on their part.

They are very committed and have a much-exaggerated vision of themselves, masking deep weakness and shame. Nurture with praise and admiration, and are deeply hurt by criticism and even honest comment. Good comments or constructive criticism threaten their self-confidence and can lead to anger. All these qualities interfere with the ability of narcissists to make healthy relationships. People associated with narcissists may feel lonely and tired when trying to support their peers and give them advice about their feelings.

Significance of Understanding and Dealing with Narcissism

Growing up under the supervision of narcissist parent is emotionally and mentally torturing. The damage is also complex and permanent and has followed us for decades and is destroying not only our own inner sense but also our sense of where we are in the world. These effects can be overcome, but we need to know how to detect patterns of toxicity and self-destruction that keep us in fear and are limited and live on less than we deserve.

The growing victim of narcissism does not mean that you have to live forever like this. Whether your parent is still in your life or just the remnants of your past, you can free yourself from the shadows and create your own healing path. Start by setting limits using these realistic techniques and you will discover the (beautiful) original and beautiful person who has been hiding for all these years. The healing work required by the children raised by narcissist parent may include many things.

At first, they may feel difficult, if not impossible to understand, and not believe that you can actually establish this type of relationship in your personal life. Well start your relationship with your therapist and let him show you what is possible in the healthiest relationships. The therapist should be a well-qualified specialist who can help you to live in a healthy way. Over time, this can affect who you attract in your personal life.

It is very important to learn more about narcissistic behavior. The initial and main step in the recovery process is to recognize that there is something wrong with the parents' behavior. Nobody can recover from something he refuses to admit. Most of the narcissistic parents choose the favorite child; who behaves as if he/she walked on water. Other children are often treated as inferior by comparison, neglecting, depreciation and ignoring.

From time to time, parents change their preferences based on the child's performance. The key to remember is that narcissistic parents see the child as an extension of themselves, limiting success and rejecting the child who has failed. Once you have recognized narcissism, it is important to inform yourself about the disorder and its effects on the entire family system. Narcissism is both biology and environment. So, there are probably narcissists or other personality disorders in the family. The environment can extract narcissism in children who were reinforced in the 18th. Discover the signs and symptoms of narcissism to take the right measures.

How to Treat Narcissist Patients?

Most of us love our parents, no matter the circumstances, we maintain our need to love and check their side. A narcissistic parent is not able to love you unconditionally as we all deserve to be loved within our families. However, you can still love your narcissistic parent. Filled with pain and anger, you can also empathize with your parents' NDP. You can also be cruel to your parents or very familiar with the feeling of love.

Almost all the narcissistic parents are emotionally in need, but these parents show ownership more openly than others. This is a father or a mother you have to take care of her emotionally which is a losing intention for the child.

The feelings of the child are neglected and it is unlikely that the child will get the same nutrition as expected from parents. In case your parents have some of these, it's very important to keep in mind that they are not narcissists by birth. Perhaps they had insurmountable obstacles to receiving love and compassion as children. It does not take away your pain. Child abuse cannot be tolerated. However, good knowledge helps to deepen understanding.

After knowing the narcissistic symptoms and what are the circumstances that can make someone narcissistic, it's time to discuss how to treat that person. This can be difficult, especially in a relationship, friendship or even in a family member where someone has narcissistic symptoms. They can be fun to hang out with and you don't want to stop connecting yourself with them. However, you can also start feeling unhappy if you feel constantly inferior or small.

Try to stay positive and use the best healing methods to treat yourself if you are raised by narcissist parents. For narcissists, relationships dominate the issue of personal development.

They tend to look for other attentive and admiring people. As a result, the other parent may have adapted to the narcissistic life by learning how to improve the flow of inflated information, with protection and claiming to have been criticized. Need and helpless can experience the needs of the child as a burden. Worse still, the child's demands can trigger the resentment by reminding the narcissistic parent of what they did not receive as a child.

You should know when you need help. Regular treatment with a person who has a narcissistic personality can affect his mental and physical health. If you experience symptoms of anxiety, depression, or unexplained physical illness, consults your health care provider first. Once the analysis is complete, you can request referrals from other services, such as therapists and support groups. Connect with family and friends and turn your help system on. There is no need to go alone.

How Growing up with Narcissistic Parents can

Affect you?

The main problem faced by narcissistic parents is that, in order to teach their children, they already forget to recognize and support the sense of autonomy of their children. Instead, the child feels a lot of pressure from his parents. They may be afraid of failure and have the feeling that they will not be good enough.

Their insecurity can cause them to become narcissistic, seeking attention and obtaining the necessary approval to prove that they are doing well. Parents who give up their lives enter the world of children instead of inviting them to participate in their lives. Because children learn, for example, the absence of a fulfilling father gives him the feeling of having to take care of his father. They must make them happy and support them. It is a heavy burden for the child and is hurting situation throughout their life.

They can re-establish this dynamic in their relationships and search for someone who amplifies the ego or strikes it in such a way as to support their great attitudes towards themselves. They can also find people who use them, like their parents, to feel good about them.

These dynamics can be detrimental to an adult, but they are semi-moral and imposed on the child. When we refuse to see our children as separate individuals, we expect all our negative and critical attitudes towards ourselves. We can try to compensate for the mistakes of our parents or recreate destructive patterns for our childhood.

In any case, we lose the mark with our children. We do not match their unique needs and are not sensitive to their true desires. By distinguishing ourselves from our past, we can see our children better than separated from ourselves. Only then can we offer them true love rather than a fantasy connection. Only then can we appreciate our children for who they are and help them reach their full potential.

The growth of the narcissistic child can be a shock for all children. Although the narcissistic child needs love, affection, flexibility, and encouragement, he receives a permanent message that his needs are neither reasonable nor humiliating. It is a worrying dynamic that can affect a child for the rest of his life. The healing of childhood wounds of the narcissistic parent takes time, but healing and redefinition of love and acceptance are possible if steps are taken to eliminate children from toxic environments.

Why it is Important to Treat Narcissist Parents?

Parents who seem to offer something to their children by immersing themselves in the interests, activities, and achievements of their children often take more than they give. Narcissistic parents feed their ego through the exploits of their children.

Although the process is somewhat unconscious, they are looking for ways to live their child. It is rare for the narcissistic parents to reveal this about themselves, their investment in the success of their children is obvious to most people around them, but this attitude is careless and often has uncomfortable consequences Narcissistic parents pose another problem, even if they seem to support the achievements of their children, but they often have the impression that they are competing with one another.

They want their children's successes to be reflected and attracted by their attention but at the same time, they do not want their children to hide them, so narcissistic parents do not upkeep a healthy sense of confidence in their children, as an alternative they will draw care and attention to themselves by through their children in an indifferent and harmful way, the only use these parents have for their child is to think of narcissistic parents who often suffer from low self-esteem and live through their children to catch up with them.

Narcissistic parents communicate excessively with their children because of their benefit. They want their children's performances to be reflected in them. The reasons are complex. Parents can try to compensate for what they think is their own disadvantages. They can count on the success of their child to strengthen themselves. In doing so, they did not perceive their son as a unique and independent individual. They refuse to realize that their child is separated from them by their thoughts, feelings, and desires.

The narcissistic parent tends to focus on the achievements of their children. Often they do it because something is missing. They can try to use your child to fill a void they feel in themselves.

Parents who lead busy lives have many interests, close relationships and emotions, often offer more to their children than those who give up everything to be with them. Although they do it in the name of love, they do not realize that their concept of love is really distorted. People mostly confuse the feelings of love with passionate hunger. Parents who believe they give their children constant attention do not know how much they throw or drain.

When a person feels a need or a passion for his child, it may be a harbinger that they take more than they give in their relationship. If a parent feels that their child is filling in a part of it, for example, it is their only source of joy, it can be an additional warning that they are suffering emotional hunger for their child. Love is about offering support, affection and encouragement. On the other hand, emotional hunger provides the opposite.

How Narcissism Interfere with Parents?

Narcissists know how to do everything: they take all the air out of the room. Their deep need for attention and praise responds to the needs of all.

Without control, the narcissism of the father prevails over the feelings of the child. Narcissistic parents personally take every feeling or action of their children.

These parents are easily angry when the child does not agree with them or does not reflect them. Narcissistic parents are prone to praise and admiration as fuel, which makes them very sensitive to criticism. Thus, children learn what these emotional minefields are, trying not to provoke this anger, or worse, for their parents to withdraw their love.

The children will also notice the emotional weakness of their parents. Acknowledge their parents or try to be an ideal reflection of them. They hope that caring for a parent helps them stay healthy so they can look after them in the end. With all the attention given to parents, these children may lose touch with their own feelings and needs

Why Being Raised by a Narcissist Parent is so damaging?

Narcissistic parents may have grown up this way because of what they loved about their parents. Thus passes from generation to generation until one person of the generation decides to break the circle in a conscious and deliberate way. The effects of childhood emotional abuse and neglect are well documented. We know that children have basic developmental needs that involve constant attachment, reflection; harmony and positive respect from key leaders who help them build a stable, consistent and positive sense of self and help them learn safe relationships.

We also know that when children do not receive it routinely, or when they receive static emphysema or repeated experiences of unsafe attachment, lack of empathy, or apparent hostility from caregivers it affects them in many ways. Unfortunately, parents with NDP have almost hostile personal traits to provide their children with what they need for their emotional and mental development and their prosperity.

It is wondered that what happens to the development of child personality when they live under the supervision of the narcissistic parent. You have to deal with many toxic effects when you are raised by a narcissist parent. Here are some of the most common effects that have damaging effects on you

- **Post-Traumatic Stress Disorder (PTSD)**

Narcissistic abuse and education often go hand in hand, resulting in traumatized children suffering from psychological trauma. When they abuse us, we are concerned to try to avoid abuse in order to start living in a state of constant anxiety and vigilance, numbing our emotions so as not to imagine life after the next moment.

- **Echoism**

Narcissistic parents who get angry without warning or collapse whenever a child dares to express their need to force sensitive children to occupy as little space as possible as if all expectations were selfish. Ecologists fight for voice and often find themselves with a very narcissistic parent.

- **Severe independence**

Adventurous children can respond to narcissistic parent by abandoning their emotional affinity, believing that no one can be trusted. This is impossible, of course, and can easily generate panic. Instead, children with more sensitive moods can become obligatory and self-serving caregivers, as if the only way to take advantage of parenting was indirectly to give others the warmth and care they had never enjoyed.

- **Chronic guilt and disgust**

Children yearn for love, but this love is hardly received by a father obsessed with him. Because they cannot meet their inherent needs for affection, these children often seek absences by sacrificing self-respect on the altar of narcissism and their parents.

• Strong Narcissism

Our parents are our role models and first indicators of the type of person we must train. Seeing a father who is always the smartest, smartest and most complete person in the room will lead him to do more of the same thing, often leading to adults who have a terrible temperament and stubborn cruelty that makes them uncomfortable in the room.

• Obsessed with the happiness of others

Sympathy is a blessing these days, but it can be a problem also. The children who grow up as sufferers of narcissistic parents mostly become possessed with creating happiness around them, often harming their own needs. Some do not even like their own needs, saying they do not deserve a burden.

• Unsafe attachment

When we are neglected, abused or removed from the emotions of our parents, we may wonder how safe we are with anyone in our lives. This can lead to an unsafe installation or an avoidance facility in which we fear not to like excluding people or building walls that prevent them from approaching,

• Damaging individuality

The child who knows that his parent does not love them is the child who knows he is the only person in the world who can trust him. When our parents are absorbed in their own worlds, we become adults who believe that no one can be trusted. However, the problem is that no one is an island and we need the love, compassion, and support of others to maintain our happiness and well-being.

Symptoms of Narcissistic Parent

A narcissistic parent can be defined as a person who lives through disregarding of competition with offspring. In general, the narcissistic father considers the independence of the child (including adult children) as a threat, forcing the children to exist under the parents, with unreasonable expectations. In a relationship of narcissistic kinship, a child is not loved for himself or for himself. Although some parents may have some of the following characteristics at one time or another, which may not be a big problem, the narcissistic parent tends to satisfactorily live many of the following while remaining largely unaware (or inspired). These behaviors affect the offspring of the individual.

Symptoms of narcissistic personality disorder may include many things like they believe that you are superior to others and that you cannot only communicate with the people who are superior to you. They may exaggerate their talents and achievements with others. They may have great importance for themselves and show the inability to listen and worry about the feelings and needs of others. Here are some symptoms of a narcissistic parent

• Lives through one's child

Most parents want their children to succeed. However, many narcissistic parents have set their expectations to meet their selfish dreams as well as needs. Instead of feeding a child who nurtures and appreciates his thoughts, emotions, and goals, the offspring is just an extension of the parents' personal desires, as the child's personality diminishes.

• Neglect

In some cases, the narcissistic father may choose to focus primarily on his self-absorption concerns, which for narcissists is more exciting than parenting. These activities can provide stimulation, validation and personal importance that you dream about, both for work obsession, for social extravagance, for adventure and for hobbies. Leave the child to the other parent or alone.

• **Own your achievements**

Whenever someone praises your exploits, your parents jump at your eyes and immediately attract attention. For example, if someone congratulates you on winning a football, your parents will come and say something like; yes it is because I invested on him. They like to live in limelight and try to steal it from you.

How you can Deal with Narcissistic Parent?

We cannot ignore how significant it is for the parents to give good lifestyle to their children. There are many children who are dealing with narcissistic parents and things can be very difficult if they are not informed or advised on how to handle this situation. Narcissism is a serious personality disorder where a person attaches more importance to his or her personal interests than to others. A narcissistic parent may be completely unresponsive to their child's feelings and does not understand their needs.

One of the oldest and common clichés about raising children is that we begin to receive new respect and compassion for our parents as we raise our children. You may have already felt that your parents were strangers, that you had exceptional fun and that your needs did not interest you, but that you did not have your children alone, you began to understand the meaning of indifference. In short, something in the experience of raising children has broken deprivation and rationalization for long periods of annoying understanding that you are a victim of childhood mistreatment. According to the clinical psychologist's experience, although these reactions are of great concern, they can lay the groundwork for healing.

Here are some of the best ways you can deal with Narcissistic Parents

• Do not blame your narcissistic parents

Many victims of narcissistic parents are obsessed with the feeling of inadequacy resulting from innumerable verbal aggression against them, children and adults. Some of these adult children decide to break their relationship with the narcissistic father. They can no longer tolerate this kind of verbal abuse and the complicity of their parents with other family members to destroy their reputation.

• Acceptance and pain

In many cases, narcissist mother is the daughter of the narcissistic parent. She never grew up in the true sense of the word; she never realized that the world was not limited to it. The important thing to remember is that your problem is not your problem.

Agree to be your mother as she is, and no one can do anything about it. It can never be reasonable, balanced or caring for someone else. Allow yourself to cry for that. Renouncing the false hope of having a better relationship with her will relieve you.

• Don't try to change them

Confronting your behavior will not help you achieve the results you are looking for. Your mother or father believes that the whole world revolves around her/him. Live in a bubble where they can do nothing wrong. He is not capable of self-reflection. Narcissus cannot see your achievements. It is important to remember that you did not do anything wrong, despite what led to its ratification. Do not try to fend for yourself. Remember that you are as good as you, even if your parent rejects you.

• Low contact

You must move away from your parent in such cases.

Distance is very important for your mental well-being. Avoid approaching as soon as possible. Limit the time you spend with. Make sure you communicate with your own terms and be very firm on your limits. If you are minor and cannot move yet, keep a conversation to a minimum. Seeing her physically does not mean you have to share with her. There is no link: in some cases, walking and not being contacted may be the only way to heal. Remember that it is about healing and moving forward in your life.

The most significant thing to keep in mind is to stay calm. Remember that they are seriously ill and cannot be avoided. It is very difficult to cut off contact with someone as important as your father or mother. Some recommend financial support without emotional involvement. In this way, you know that they are cared for and that all their needs are met. You must really accept and move on.

How You Can Heal Yourself?

Origin of your family is not something that defines you, but it is your true self. Learn to become aware of their true nature and calm the little child's heart by practicing certain practices to calm the mind through guided meditation and simple yoga emphasizing the breathing through the nose so to stimulate the sedative part of the nervous system. Start your creativity with the music you love the art of anyway, dance, sing, write automatically and find ways to be part of a very small nature every day.

If you are raised by a narcissistic parent, healing yourself is very important as it has a positive effect on all other close relationships in a person's life. The partial perception of reality imposed by the narcissistic parent on the child can have adverse consequences for adulthood at work and at home. Lack of self-confidence, reduced abuse, excessive anxiety, fear-based reactions, and obsessive thinking are common among narcissistic adult children.

Here are 8 things you can do to heal yourself.

Educate Yourself About Narcissism

Accept That Your Narcissist Parent Won't Change

Recognize the Roles in Your Family

Assert Boundaries

Don't Blame Yourself

Stop Hurting Yourself

Be Aware of Your Attractions with Narcissists

Treat Yourself for Narcissistic "Fleas"

You can help yourself in many ways. Take the right steps right now and you can take yourself now on the path to healing.

1. Educate yourself about Narcissism

If you realize that one of your parents is narcissistic, you should continue to recognize what you are dealing with. Explore the internet for good resources. Read, join discussion boards, and watch shows and movies that have narcissistic characters. Besides this, take appointment from a therapist who is able to understand narcissism. Educating yourself will help you to understand what has happened and what you need to do to overcome the toxic influence of your family.

Whether through books or by the help of a professional, you may need to start to know what narcissism is and how it can appear in parenthood, as well as than its potential effects. The first step in any healing process is to educate people about who they are, and it seems that the psychological education of narcissists can be very helpful when you start to understand your past. The goal is to help him understand what he is facing and to say that the way he was treated is not his fault. Read books and watch movies and TV shows that will make you feel scared and laugh. It is necessary to separate yourself emotionally from the parent who has taken control of your life so you can start looking at your beautiful body. Also, accept that they are not likely to change.

2. Accept that your narcissistic parent would not change

Accepting the fact that your narcissist parent probably does not change is a very difficult thing. If narcissism is perceived in his life as a means of personally advancing towards a great health problem, however, you must assume that it will not. If narcissism is your parent that you cannot completely eliminate from your life, accept it as it is. They will not change. They do not believe there is something wrong with them. They think you are the problem. Trying to avoid the fact that this person will never give you what you need is not something difficult, but it works as a fuel for the fire. Alternative, acceptance is difficult but it is the key.

Accept that they will never change. Accept not to receive love from them. You accept the fact that you deserve love and that you can get it from someone else. Others will love you too. Narcissists rarely change, and if they behave more satisfactorily, it will probably be a scheming maneuver. Keeping hope that the parents will finally give you the unconditional love you crave throughout your life is normal, but it is a mistaken dream that makes you vulnerable to further abuse and prevents you from getting over these things.

3. Recognize the roles in your family

Each family has dynamics and roles played by different members. In some of the families, there is a culprit. While in others, there is a special child. There are various fluid roles in a typical family unit, but they are always organized by the narcissists and not always in favor of the individuals concerned. Narcissistic parents keep control of their families by creating a division between these families. They move away from their fellow children and separate siblings from each other by choosing them at the same time as villains and a victim, creating a confusing system that makes it difficult to know which path is available when it comes to the roles of the family. Pay careful attention to family roles and watch them when used to create a power seat, and restrict roles to others.

The best way to defend against this type of attack is to create a united front, but this requires communication and cohesion. They achieved mutual understanding and unity as to which part to interpret and why, and tried to reinforce each other rather than give in to the controversial oratory used by the aggressor to stay in place. If there is no one in your family you can trust, protect yourself from your contact with those who are destroying you and your family so you can control it.

4. Assert boundaries

Set boundaries with narcissist parents in your life or with those who may be more comfortable and attentive. Learning healthy boundaries and knowing how to adjust them with others is essential for those who are recovering from narcissistic parents. Narcissistic parents are often absorbed by themselves. They may think that they have the right to go where they want, to go through personal things or to tell you what you should feel. They can give you unwanted tips and take the credits of your achievements or they may stress you to discuss your special things in a public setting. They may not aware of personal space, so they try to cross many boundaries. Most of the time, they do not even see them. That's why you should be very clear about the limits that interest you.

As a narcissistic survivor, you are an objector and are not respected as someone who has your identity. The narcissist tells him what he thinks and feels and insists that he conforms to his story of genuineness no matter how false, harmful or absurd it is. One of the important and difficult things you should do is set healthy limits. Understanding what it means and feeling comfortable can take a lot of time and practice for a narcissistic child. The first place to start is a narcissistic father and possibly with other members of the family.

5. Don't blame yourself

When narcissists commit a mistake, they have a habit to blame others. When you are wrong, they will always blame you. But when they succeed, they will always cite their part in the success. When you succeed, they describe it by chance or reduce it by designating failure at other times. People suffering from narcissism tend to be distracted and camouflaged. Like children trapped in a jar of candy, they may try to confuse, minimize, intimidate or avoid responsibility for their actions.

Pay close attention to their actions instead of their words. Words often attempt to get rid of you and make you feel small or doubtful when you feel good. In general, your arguments should not be taken seriously until they have been answered, because if you refute this argument, you can simply suggest another argument. When they are abusive, manipulative or inmates, look at them for what they are.

They use you to avoid their problems and meet their needs. They may feel empowered to do so. It's not healthy. No one has the right to abuse or use someone else. Never ever blame yourself especially if you are a culprit in your family. You will automatically blame yourself for things beyond your responsibility and control.

Narcissists are experts in the transformation and guilt of others. If you are angry and defending yourself, they will attack you. If they hit you, force them to do it. One of the best ways to break the unhealthy dynamics of your family is to stop accusing yourself of never being responsible or being wrong.

6. Stop hurting yourself

In addition to not blaming you, you may need to disable self-abuse habits. As a person who grew up in a narcissistic family, you are subject to risky, self-punishing and self-appeasing, but devastating behaviors, such as drug abuse and addiction, self-harm and emotional digging. Your destructive self-destructive behavior is an internal level of narcissistic abuse that develops there, which is the opposite of the pain of your narcissus. By adopting such behavior, you continue to grant yourself narcissistic power. You also aggravate the emotional and physiological trauma you are already experiencing. It can be very difficult to break the patterns of addiction and self-harm, so ask for help and support from people who understand the dynamics of narcissism.

7. Be aware of your attractions with the narcissists

Many adult narcissistic children are likely to be attracted to relationships with narcissists not belonging to their original family, including peers, friends as well as bosses. It hurts, but it is not a shame.

 Repeating the past so that we learn from it is a way to heal the mind and body. So be careful. If you are engaged in unhealthy relationships, forgive yourself and keep going. Only about 6% of people have NDP. There are a lot of non-narcissists, so go for it. So the narcissists can be an attraction. However, we usually use the word in a negative light. Indeed, the most important characteristic of narcissists is that, even if they have high self-esteem, they have a weak opinion of others and that it is not generally a healthy characteristic.

The most important point is you must distinguish between the specific characteristics of the people who attract you and the advantage of neglecting others so that they feel good because, although they are generally related, they do not always go together. There are people who are incredible, fun and comfortable enough not to have to interfere with others to prove it. Find out why you think it's inseparable and see what has affected your mind. When people are told repeatedly that they are impressive and necessary, it will take a lot of emotional maturities not to fall into the bubble of superiority. So it can be strange. Go find them.

8. **Treat yourself for narcissistic "fleas"**

Narcissistic children are likely to acquire some narcissistic characteristics, also known as narcissistic fleas. Some become narcissistic in their own right, but many only perpetuate certain behaviors that can be overcome with interest and practice. See for yourself what motivates you? What does this narcissistic father remind you of your mother? Are you angry? Do you search for   control or attention through manipulation or guilt?

The best revenge is a life that has lived well. Treat yourself well and make peace in your own life. You cannot help with the way you are raised, but you can control how you act now and how you raise your children. There are some symptoms of fleas

They occasionally snap and become aggressive with the attacker, and can hit him.

Usually calm, but sometimes insulting and shouting, they often feel out of control.

They generally treat the differences calmly but then participate in negative aggressive behaviors, such as the destruction of the abuser's property when they are not present.

The truth is that when we take the fleas of narcissist's parents, we are already implementing inappropriate coping strategies.

Millions of people have narcissists in their families. You are not alone. These tips and many other tips can help you break with the emotional control around you and many others. You may be surprised by the energy, the hobbies and the inner peace that you can get. Of course, it is not easy but it is possible if you try to deal with this problem very carefully.

Verdict

The word narcissism has been tossed much around our celebrity-driven and self-obsessed culture and it is often being used to describe the one who looks like full of themselves or excessively vain. But in terms of psychology, it could not be defined as self-love, not for a genuine sort at least. It is because when it comes to excess then it would be better to say that people are suffering from a disorder are in love with a grandiose and an idealized image of themselves.

It is because these are in love with themselves to the extent that they are unable to see the goodness of other people around them. Such people are truly occupied with an exaggerated self-image precisely and even these feelings are allowing them to avoid their own deep feelings of self-insecurity. Narcissism is also present in parents and maternal narcissism is something which can affect kids the most.

The effect of maternal narcissism has the ability to create significant emotional damage to the kids which are being raised by such mothers. They have been raised up with a thought that there is their fault in every situation or they are not enough good to compete in the world.

So, once if you have understood the fact that your mother is a narcissist then this is the time to do some things for yourself to set up healthy relationships in an effective way. Whatever the origin and reality of your family are, you must think about to move on with your own life or to set boundaries. It is because it is never later to go towards better things, to process your feelings or work to heal the damages. Even if you are still living as a miner in your home there are multiple ways by which you can help yourself in a better way.

Although narcissists more often violate the boundaries but you have to do this difficult job of establishing healthy boundaries. Understand the true meanings of things. Although getting comfortable with doing this takes much time and effort but the chances of positive results would become higher with consistent efforts.

More importantly, stop blaming yourself. It is because this is the most common practice which has been observed in the kids raised under maternal narcissism. Therefore, one of the most important and best way to break unhealthy influence is to stand up for yourself for the things which were never your responsibility. However, it is highly important for you to educate yourself about narcissism especially if you are new to this concept. You must think about to know more details in this regard. It is because this ultimately will help you to find better healing solutions.

About the Author

Alma S.Bailey , Phd is a psychologist and writer. She has over two decades of experience and has worked with hundreds of individuals and couples on a wide range of relationship and intimacy issues.

In addition to running her private practice, Dr.Alma S.Bailey , has lectured at several universities and conducts workshops on a variety of marital and relationship topics. Her relationship advice has appeared on television, radio, and in national magazines.

.

Made in United States
Orlando, FL
26 May 2023

33484291R10098